DEVOTIONS TO MY PEOPLE

31 DAYS TO BOOST YOUR DEVOTION LIFE IN RECOVERY

ANTHONY TORRES

Devotions To My People
Copyright © 2022 by Anthony Torres

Paperback ISBN 978-0-578-36402-5

*This devotion book is dedicated
to my beloved sister, Sonya Baca:*

Heaven's Gain

As the rain begun to fall and the thunder begin to rumble, losing you was setting in as we all begin to crumble.
You are home.

No more sleepless nights, you can now put down your burdens. Because my sister, there is no more hurting.
You are home.

Even though here it was dark from the clouds and wet from the pouring rain, as we kissed you goodbye all we felt was pain.
You are home.

As the wind begin to blow from the north to south you went about your normal route to *his* gates, I know your spirit was eager and you couldn't wait.
You are home

Tell me! How beautiful is it? How in awe were you? As he wrote, *he* makes all things *new*! And Sonya that's *you*!
You are home.

How did it feel to hear *his* voice? With a lump in your throat I know you rejoiced. Tell us, how was your embrace? How did it feel to walk on that fresh grass with no shoes, it's not like the grass down here that still has dew?
You are home.

I wonder how your heart felt when you heard, "Sonya."
As you looked around to see all your loves. Oh look
you just saw a flying dove! As tears of joy began to fall,
he wiped your eyes and said to all,
"You're home!"

We will miss you down here, but we have to keep
going with Jesus in our hearts. Dodging all those fiery
darts. So when it's our time, we can hear you call our
name, and *we* will feel the same. So we can hear
"*You're home.*"

AND WHATEVER YOU
DO, IN WORD OR DEED,
DO EVERYTHING IN THE
NAME OF THE LORD
JESUS, GIVING THANKS
TO GOD THE FATHER
THROUGH HIM.

COLOSSIANS 3:17

DAY 1

WHAT'S A DEVOTION LIFE?

A lot of the time when I talk to people, I talk with them about their devotion life to God. Sometimes I get asked, "What is that?" and "What does that look like?" Since I have gotten straight with God, even till this day, I have had a devotion time with God. It consists of making some coffee, picking a devotion book like this one, reading one or two chapters in the Bible, and then praying while listening to worship music. After that I will get my journal and write down my goals for the day, things that are on my heart, and what I felt the Scripture was speaking to me to better my life.

This is my devotion time with God and it was something that no one taught me. I just did it. I knew I had to be a better person in this life, I knew I needed more than what my old life was giving me. I needed more of Christ in my life no matter what.

You might be saying "I don't have time for that". You will make time for things in your life that are important to you. The way I saw things early on was

3

that I would spend many mornings throwing up, or many mornings trying to find my next high. Even mornings not wanting to live. Why not shape my new mornings for God! My body now is wired where I am up early to give my start of the day to God. A devotion life to God is a disciplined life. It's a life that says, "I put you first in my day." It says, "I need your strength, wisdom, your direction for my day." Devotion is a time where we also ask for him to forgive us, or maybe their areas in our lives that we need to work on. This is a daily thing, and I truly believe we could have more delivered people from addiction, if we just live a life devoted to him. I believe that we could see a lot more people healed in their hearts if we just live a life devoted to him. More people truly finding their identity in Christ if we just live a life devoted to him.

Here is a checklist for your devotion life:
- Pick a time for devotion time
- Drink something hot (tea or coffee)
- Find a good devotion book (Once you're done with it, find others)
- Pick which book you want to read from in the Bible (Acts, John, Genesis-write down what the scripture is speaking to you about)
- Pick a worship song to listen to and pray
- Journal (write down your heart and things you want God to work in your life
- Repeat Daily

This will get you started in your devotion life with God. I promise you will feel so much better, inside and out. You will feel the presence of God like no other. He will begin to shape and mold you in his image for you to be a better man or woman for him.

Enjoy this Devotion book! I pray it blesses and helps you

WHEN JESUS SAW HIM
LYING THERE AND KNEW
THAT HE HAD ALREADY
BEEN THERE A LONG
TIME, HE SAID TO HIM,
"DO YOU WANT TO BE
HEALED?"

JOHN 5:6

DAY 2

DO YOU WANT TO
BE MADE WELL?

Recovery can be hard! But it is possible! Any-thing is possible with God. The first time I heard those words in church, I remember telling myself, "This preacher does not know what I am going through. If this God is as powerful as I heard and read, we shall see how my life plays out from here." But I stayed with it, no matter how many times I fell, and I applied so much to my new-found faith in Christ and my new life in recovery.

Let me ask you a question to start off this devo-tion, "Do you want to be made well?" I am sure you're saying, "Well of course! I am reading your book and now doing this daily devotion, and I am going to church." And that's great! But do you *really* want change? Do you really want a *new life*? I want you to write this down.

"Change always starts with sacrifice."

Are you willing to put in the work and the sacrifice you need to have a sober and clean life?"

I love this story here in John 5 because it's says "Jesus knew he already had been in that condition for a long time." So in other words, Jesus was about to test him with the same question I asked you. Do you want to be made well? Here is why. Sometimes we have been a certain way for such a long time we don't know anything else, and we are okay in our addiction. We get comfortable with it. This man had been this way for so long, making so many excuses for why he couldn't get in the pool when the angel would stir it. Does this sound familiar? Excuses for why we are not well and playing the victim mentally will keep us in our cycle of addiction longer.

Jesus was telling him, "You need to make sure you want to be made well. Because when I come in, I change all things!" I could identify with this story here, because I was okay being the drunk, the center of the party. The person who was always coked up with his snot constantly running as it dripped down his nose, while his mouth moved from side to side enjoying his high. Everyone knew what I was doing, even my family, and I was okay with it. I can tell you, back then I didn't want to be made well.

As you read this Day 2 devotion, I want you to ask yourself some questions. Now that Jesus is in your heart, how can he help you be made well in your life today? What are believing God for?

Write it down here:

I am telling you that you can really do this. Here I am today, 11 years and 6 months clean and sober. I am telling you, I want to be made well every single day. But what Jesus told the man next should encourage you. In verse 9 he said, "Rise, take up your bed and walk." Immediately the man was made well, took up his bed, and walked.

Friend, Rise up today! Get walking! And be made well! The *only* thing that is stopping you is *you*. Be well from your past, be well in your heart, and be well in your life.

Thoughts & Notes

IF WE CONFESS OUR
SINS, HE IS FAITHFUL
AND JUST TO FORGIVE US
OUR SINS AND TO
CLEANSE US FROM ALL
UNRIGHTEOUSNESS

1 JOHN 1:9

DAY 3

FORGIVING YOURSELF

Why is it hard to forgive yourself? Because the truth and reality is, people will *always* bring up your past and not let you forget. They bring up the hurt you caused them. They always want to take you back to the past, no matter how far you have come or how happy you are. It's like a dagger in your side. You're always reminded with every twist as it pierces your side. When they really want to do some damage to your spirit, they pull the knife out. They will always want to take you back to where God pulled you out from. My favorite saying is, "I don't live *there* anymore." In other words I don't live in 2005 anymore, nor do I live in 2009. I live in to-day. My thought process is, *you* can stay there, but I *choose* to continue to move forward.

Now, I'm not justifying the hurt and pain you caused others. Nor am I dismissing their feelings. But somewhere in your life, you have to move *for-ward* and quit going backwards because of what's being said and forgive yourself. At the end of the

13

day, you have to know according to this scripture that God is faithful in forgiving you. As long as you're *right* with God and forgiven, that's all that matters. The healing must begin in your life.

We can't say it's too hard to keep going with the past being brought up. Listen! As long as you're alive, the past will always be brought up. Just the other day, someone brought up something that they thought happened seventeen years ago with me. Remember, I don't live there anymore, and either should you.

The *point* of this Day 3 devotion, is that you have to truly forgive yourself in order for healing and recovery to begin. How many people have relapsed because the past has gotten the best of them? They moved backwards instead of forward. It took me a long time to be able to look at myself in the mirror again, but I had to forgive myself. When I read this scripture for the first time, it really was a comfort for my heart and soul. *You mean to tell me all the bad stuff I did or say, that I was forgiven?* Yes! That's what that scripture meant, not just for the past but for the future as well.

I made my amends with people that accepted my apologies. I said sorry to all the people that I hurt and did wrong. I had to leave their emotions, and hatred towards me, even their revenge in God's hands. I even had to leave the emotions that my kids had towards me in God's hands. Listen! You just do your part, and let God do his. You cannot compete with other's thoughts towards you, or change their minds about you. This will leave you tired and stressed out. If we are not careful, we will allow other's thoughts towards us, or even their emotions, to become poison to our healing souls. The past is a *horrible* place to visit when you try to relive it every day. You cannot allow yourself to re-visit an area that God is slowly pulling you out of. Forgiving yourself is so crucial in your recovery.

So right now, know that you're forgiven by God for everything that you have said or done. It's a *clean* slate, every day of your life. But you have to walk in that forgiveness and believe it's for you to-day and forgive yourself. You can't change the past or even go back there. Jesus can! Let him handle that, and you live in the *now* with a heart to forgive yourself. Your spirit will thank you, and your heart will beat again. Forgive yourself!

SO THEN EACH OF US

WILL GIVE AN ACCOUNT

OF HIMSELF TO GOD

ROMANS 14:12

DAY 4

CAN YOU EMBRACE RESPONSIBILITY?

Let's be honest, taking responsibility is hard for us. And I wonder were this comes from. Was it somewhat of a learned behavior that we developed over the years? Was it something that we saw as an example from our parents or others? I am sure it could come from a lot of things. But not taking responsibility for our actions or words does more damage to us than we know. We just spin in a cycle of never fully making things better in our lives. We can spend years blaming others instead of seeing what we need to fix. Here is something I really want you to think about, everyone sees it except us. But not anymore, today is a new day for you. A day you take *full* responsibilities. You know why? Because you're not that man or woman anymore.

Life is not fair. It never has been. And as long as we are alive, it never will be. Sometimes we get the short end of the stick, we get cards that are not fair and we have to deal with it. Sometimes our life is even altered because of our own decision making. But fair or not, you give God what you can't control. Give him that unfairness. And you, my dear friend, embrace responsibility of your own actions. This is how you grow in life and in recovery. It's easy to have a pity party and play the blame game. But when you embrace responsibility, not only do you take back your life, you also take back your *character* that you are now building on. You start to slowly dig yourself out of that hole that you got yourself into. You slowly start to get your life back. And you start to see *wins* in your life.

Here are some easy ways to do this.
- Get rid of *pride* and swallow it. Pride is *killer* in taking responsibility.
- *Never* be in embarrassed. We all mess up.
- *Stop* blaming others where you are.
- Own up to what you said or did. It's okay to say sorry.
- Embrace where you are at right now and see this challenging time as a chance to grow more in your spirit.
- Let that guilt *go*. It's not yours to carry anymore.
- Make amends with others. If they don't accept it, you did your part, *move on.*

I'm proud of you! Taking responsibility is hard.

Thoughts & Notes

But you, take courage! Do not let your hands be weak, for your work shall be rewarded.

2 Chronicles 15:7

DAY 5

WHAT ARE YOU WRITING DOWN?

One of the first things I started to do when I was in recovery was *write things down*. My goals, my dreams, my *action* plan in getting myself together. Thinking about what you need to do is one thing. Writing it down is another and here is why. What you write down, is what you own! You see it, you know what you have to do. I would cross out things that I would accomplish and then I would add more things I needed to get done. Consider it like a play-book to get you where you need to be. Even till this day I write things down, I am still doing my best to stay constantly focused on the task and mission of staying clean and sober. Just because I have been in recovery a long time doesn't mean I stop doing what's been working for me. That is why I am in recovery for a long time. I am still doing what is working for me even though so many years have gone by. Most times, people are in recovery for a year or two, then think, "I can stop working on what I have been doing." Then they find themselves back in addiction again. Somewhere in their journey, they stopped writing down what mattered to them.

Don't stop writing, don't stop dreaming, and don't stop reaching for your goals. Keep working. Keep those hands busy every single day in your recovery. Keep your mind sharp and alert. Put that pen to paper and believe every day for a great life!

You have to ask yourself every day, "What am I writing down?" Ask yourself "What am I working on that I'm writing down?" We cannot stay idle. I believe it is a killer to our recovery. Sooner or later, idle days will catch up to us and we will get discouraged and go back to what we knew. Addiction. Get the journal out and start writing. Stay focused on the duties and task at hand. Let's go!

22

Thoughts & Notes

AND HE SAID TO HIM, "YOU SHALL LOVE THE LORD YOUR GOD WITH ALL YOUR HEART AND WITH ALL YOUR SOUL AND WITH ALL YOUR MIND. [38] THIS IS THE GREAT AND FIRST COMMANDMENT

MATTHEW 22:37-38

DAY 6

JESUS HAS TO BE FIRST

I remember when I first became a Christian. I just went to God with the big things of life while I struggled with the small things. It took me awhile to understand that he cares about everything in my life and he wants to be the *full* center of everything that I do, big or small. He wants to hear from us. Like going to him with things such as, "God give me your wisdom today" or "Give me your strength."

But it goes deeper than that a lot of the time in our addiction. We did our will, our want in life. And, well, we know how that turned out for us! But this new life is different now. It's his will for our lives with everything. Does he want us to get this job? Or this house? Or even be in this relationship that we are in? If we are not careful, our wants will override his will. We will fall back in love with things he has pulled us out of. Even till this day, I ask of God, "If this is not in your will, shut this door immediately." I have done my best to get into a habit of asking him to help me with day to day life. Whether it's a conversation or a decision I need to make. I also do my best to make it a habit to pray over everything I do. What this does is put him at the center of attention in our everyday life. I look back and wonder how I could have ever lived without him. I sure did for almost twenty-eight years of my life. It got me nowhere good, just in a pit of hell and addiction in a life I was not happy with. When we put Jesus first, it really makes all the difference in our recovery and our life.

Whenever I see these men that I mentor begin to fall off the wagon again, my first question is, "Where is God in all this?" Most of the time they tell me, "I lost sight of who God was in my life, I stopped putting him first." My response is, "Get back up and put him first." He has to be, if you and I are going to continue in this journey of recovery. Has he been first since you started this journey of being sober and clean? And is he still first today? This a good question to ask yourself. And if he isn't, then today is a good day to start. Not just something in our life, but everything needs to come under the Lordship of Christ.

Thoughts & Notes

AND I AM SURE OF THIS,
THAT HE WHO BEGAN A
GOOD WORK IN YOU WILL
BRING IT TO COMPLETION
AT THE DAY OF JESUS
CHRIST.

PHILIPPIANS 1:6

DAY 7

BE PATIENT

What I see a lot in recovery is people who give up too quickly. It is like it's in our nature to war within ourselves to either keep going in this new life or get discouraged and go backwards. Get this in your spirit, your emotions must never trump God's promises for your life. I'm not here *just because*. I am here *because* even till this day I fight every single day in my discouragement in my life. The devil wants to take me out more now than he did eleven years ago. And he wants to take you out also. If he can destroy the man, he kills the legacy. If he destroys the woman, he rips the family apart. But we must fight back to not give up. We have to fight back knowing God is who he says he is, and believing the promises that he has for your life. We can't get discouraged and give up too quickly before we see Gods blessings in our lives.

Our emotions will always take our minds to places we need to get out of. Things like, "It's always going to be this way," or, "You're never going to have a good life." The best thing for you to do is stay still and do your part in being committed in your recovery and let God do his job. What I have learned in my life is this, we are on God's time table; he is not on ours. But his timing is perfect, we just can't get discouraged.

That work that he begun to do in you, he will see it completed. You just can't give up too quickly. Be patient in your recovery; for your life, for your career, for your relationship, and for everything that comes your way. It took years for you to make a mess out of your life. And guess what. Things will not just come together overnight. It takes being patient and watching the God who loves you, the God who never gave up on you, the God who pulled you out of the pit you were in, work in your new life. Again, you must be patient. Don't give up. Your blessings are coming!

Thoughts & Notes

31

FOR WE WALK BY FAITH,

NOT BY SIGHT

2 CORINTHIANS 5:7

DAY 8

BAD DAYS WILL COME

I think a lot of the time when people start to clean up their lives from addiction, they live in this reality that things will just start to get easier as the days go on. It's the reality that it was the addiction they were in that was keeping them in a cycle of sin and destruction. Even though there is some truth to that, as the days of being sober and clean begin, so will the hard days!

I don't say that to discourage you nor make you feel like, "Why should I continue?" You will have to fight every day for your new life, but you're not fighting alone anymore. Sober or clean, bad days will come. But we have to wire ourselves to be different in this time, because you can't run to the substance anymore to numb you, to allow you to escape your own pain. I love this scripture here because you can't operate on sight anymore, all you see what is not fair and how things are going. You will see hard days of being discouraged.

It's that internal struggle that makes you want to go back to drinking, back to drugs again. But that is not your spiritual battle anymore, your heart now belongs to Jesus and you have to keep going by faith, by his spirit, not by your flesh. Get this in your heart, starve the flesh and feed the spirit. It's in those times you have a bad day that you get off work to hopefully you can find some time to get in the presence of Jesus.

One day I was having a bad day, and I was months sober and clean and nothing was going my way that day. I felt like a failure at everything I did, I was fading very quickly. But I went home, got my Bible, and begin to pray and read Gods word and ask for him to help me. I put on some worship music and let his spirit consume me and afterwards I felt so much better. Sometimes you need to cry out, you need to let everything out that maybe you had been holding on to. Because bad days will come, but it's what you do in that moment that is going make the difference in your life. My favorite saying is, "Now is not forever." What you're going through right now is not forever, this bad day will pass. Tomorrow is a brand new day for you. But you can't just see your bad days as a setback, everyone has them. You can't see your hard days as punishment, we all get them. See them as a time to press more into the presence of Jesus. See them as an opportunity to show yourself that no matter how bad of a day you have, you can overcome. Bad days will come but get your eyes off what you see and get your eyes back on Jesus. Walk by faith and not by sight! You got this.

Thoughts & Notes

DO NOT BE DECEIVED:

"BAD COMPANY RUINS

GOOD MORALS."

1 CORINTHIANS 15:33

DAY 9

GOOD COMPANY

If there is one thing, I try to stress so much in recovery is your circle of family and friends must be *solid*. You will find out real quick in your life who is with you and who is not, who will love the new you or not. And this will continue in your life forever. You will have to guard your heart with every relationship that God brings in your life. When I started to get my life in order, I had to let go of those people that were bringing me down; those that I felt were taking me back to a place that God had taken me out of. Even till this day, I have zero room for negative people in my life. I can count how many times I have had men come along side of me and say, "I am for you, I believe in you," and, "I am here to help." They leave me and days later they are on Facebook dissing me, talking about me or talking bad about me to others on the streets.

This is what I have learned very early on; you have to surround yourself with people who will be okay with your success in your recovery or anything

37

that God does in your life. Not everyone can handle your success. I am drawn to positive people. I am drawn to people who build up others. I am drawn to people who have a genuine spirit and really want me to do good. I catch on to those things real quickly now and I keep negative people at a distance, because if you are not careful they will corrupt your recovery, they will corrupt your spirit. This is a hard area for many people, because you have formed some great relationships. And sometimes you have to let go of the old friends, and sadly sometimes even family. Your recovery is not something to gamble with, your spiritual state of mind is something that has to be so valuable that you guard your heart, your mind, and your spirit in Christ Jesus. Look at your circle today.

Look at your new friendships that you have formed. Ask yourself these key questions:

- How did they act when you succeeded?
- How did they treat you when you failed?
- How have they handled some of the lowest parts of your life?
- Do they love you with no hidden agendas?
- Have they ever thrown your past or mistakes in your face?
- Have they always supported you?
- How have they helped you in recovery?

These are question I like to ask myself now in my recovery and my new life. Some of these questions will raise red flags for you to see in people. And when that happens, it's time to guard your heart. Ask Jesus today to reveal things to you, he will. The key in your recovery, in a nut shell, is this; surround yourself with people who will support you not just in good times but in bad, and people that will help you get to your goal in recovery or life and not weigh you down. Who you allow in your circle is up to you, friend. And it's everything in recovery as I learned very early on. Not everyone is for you! Be around good company and good people that love you and that are cheering you on.

TRUST IN THE LORD
WITH ALL YOUR HEART,
AND DO NOT LEAN ON
YOUR OWN
UNDERSTANDING.
IN ALL YOUR WAYS
ACKNOWLEDGE HIM,
AND HE WILL MAKE
STRAIGHT YOUR PATHS

PROVERBS 3:5-6

DAY 10

LETTING GO OF WHAT
YOU CAN'T CHANGE

We all have a past, everyone does. Doesn't matter if people had a life of addiction or not. If all 8 billion people walking this world look back in their lives, they all have something that they are ashamed of. If only we didn't say this or that, or did something that altered our lives or those around us. The past is a horrible thing to think about, but it's a place we love to visit. We all sit around and think of the, *what ifs.* If we are not careful, we will spend so much time in the past that we cannot enjoy the present. You must give God all your pain, all your past and all your areas that you cannot go back to. Let him revisit that past and forgive and heal you, while you enjoy the now.

This scripture is so true for you today, *trust in the lord with all heart*. This means your new trust is in the creator, it's in the one who knows where you are at mentally and physically. It's a new kind of

41

trust, and it was something that I had never felt before in my life. I have trusted in myself for so long, I
have trusted my addiction, that it would do what it
was designed to do. To numb me, to help me escape my reality of life.

But this new trust is now in the Lord, you must
today let go of things that you cannot change in your
past. You must let go of things even now that you
have no control over. It allows you to release everything and say, "God I trust you with my past and
present." We can tend to hang on to things that
were never meant for us to hang on to. We have
this cycle of reliving the past, playing certain scenes
in our minds. This can hinder our recovery process.
When we don't let go of the past, when we don't let
go of things we have no control over, it's telling God
that we don't trust him. My prayer for you today is
that you will begin to trust the God that made you,
that God knows all your mistakes and failures. Yet
in the midst of that, he still loves you and wants to
be a part of your new life. Let go today and trust
him! It's so important that you lean on his understanding and not yours. When you learn to do this,
he will line up your life with his heart, and your spirit
with his will.

Thoughts & Notes

THEREFORE, IF ANYONE
IS IN CHRIST, HE IS A
NEW CREATION. THE OLD
HAS PASSED AWAY;
BEHOLD, THE NEW HAS
COME

2 CORINTHIANS 5:17

DAY 11

LEARNING THE NEW YOU

Who would have thought you could get a brand new life! In God's eyes, you're brand new. Now I know that life and even people have not made you feel like that. But you are. You now have a new spirit in you, a new heart. You now have a God-compass for your life. Learning the new you can have its challenges, but trust me when I say it's a daily thing. Even till this day being years clean and sober, I am still learning the new me. I have a saying in the church, "When you give your life to Christ, you lose the right to be the old you." Now God is not looking for perfection, but he is looking for improvement in our lives. Learning the new you will require for you to see how God is working in your life.

With your mind, you should think different. I had the mind of always being negative all the time and always seeing the worse in every situation. Learn to see things through the eyes of Christ knowing he holds your life in his hands. Even how you used to treat people. Maybe we always saw people as our enemies. It says in the Bible we are to forgive our enemies and bless them. We are to love those that are unlovable and show grace and mercy where needed. These are some tough words to read, right? Well think about it like this, there was a time we were an enemy to God, we were unlovable, *yet* God still loved us and gave us grace and mercy. See how that works?!

But it is also learning you, as a person and what you are capable of doing in your new life. I mean, who would have thought one day I would be an author or lead pastor of a church? Or a CEO of *New Life Recovery Center*? I can tell you this right now, don't put God in a box for your new life. He can do more now in your new life then you can ever imagine. Not only does he want to shape your heart, he wants to change your life. Even till this day, I don't feel worthy to be used by him, but he sees me fit. Even till this day, I ask him to find someone better, someone more educated, be he still speaks to me and says, "*Go!*" Go teach who will listen. Go preach who will receive, and be a voice for me. No matter what! I'm writing this book because he told me to.

You will have to learn your new life, your new purpose. What I try to teach men and women is to dream so big you can't deny how big your God is. You can't deny how faithful he is, how wonderful and great he is. He is a good God! Every day you're going to learn more about yourself than you ever have, your new likes, your dislikes, new hobbies, and new attitude. Because the *old* you is gone, behold the new is here. You can't go backwards while you learn the new you! I'm proud of you, keep going your brand new way. Embrace this new life, and watch God work.

REJOICE IN THE LORD

ALWAYS;

AGAIN I WILL SAY,

REJOICE

PHILIPPIANS 4:4

DAY 12

CHOOSE HAPPINESS

I have learned in life that happiness cannot be found in things or circumstances. What I mean is, most of the time we will be happy if things are going our way. Or if we have a certain amount of money in the bank account, a working car that doesn't break down all the time. All the bills are paid and everything in life is great. But my questions is, what if things don't start going our way, can we still be happy? Happiness must come from within, not from material things or life circumstances.

Can you still have the joy in your life that you need without needing things. You be surprised how many people I meet that are clean and sober and that have no joy. Your joy does not have to be in your circumstances. Your joy can be that it's another great day to be alive, it's another day you're sober and clean. I think a lot of the time in the life of an addict we have seen so much bad and hard times we don't know what happiness looks like. True happiness is knowing it's another day to make things right with God, yourself, and those around you. Happiness is waking up not dead or in the hospital due to your addictions. Happiness is the one thing I believe you can control because it comes from within your heart. I am happy today because I am alive, sober and clean. I am happy today because for once I am walking in my purpose. Whatever life throws at me I do my very best for it not to take my happiness.

I want you to choose to be happy today! You deserve it, you have overcome the odds and you're making something of your life. Be happy that you get a second chance at this life, be happy that you're going to make it. Be happy that right now *you* are in the driver seat, not your addiction anymore. Be happy you're not in jail, or waking up vomiting being hung over. Be happy that you can think straight, just be happy. Your season might not be pleasant because you're just now starting in this journey of recovery, but you must choose happiness. And in all things, rejoice in the Lord! Why? Because he saved you, he has forgiven you and even though you may find yourself alone, he is with you! Be happy today, you deserve it. It's okay to smile!

Thoughts & Notes

THEREFORE, MY
BELOVED BROTHERS, BE
STEADFAST,
IMMOVABLE, ALWAYS
ABOUNDING IN THE
WORK OF THE LORD,
KNOWING THAT IN THE
LORD YOUR LABOR IS
NOT IN VAIN

1 CORINTHIANS 15:58

DAY 13

STAY COMMITTED

Starting something in life is always the easy part, its staying with it that makes all difference in all areas of our lives. It's like how in January you have people who want to lose weight. So they spend money on some shoes and workout gear and sign up for a two year membership at the gym. First week is hard but they keep going, and now they are a month into it and things are going well. Ask those people that made that commitment in November and let's see how many people are still sticking with it. Hey, I would be the first to say I think we all have been there. But in recovery we cannot take that risk! You have all your counseling classes in order, you have a game plan. You need to stick with it.

Most of the time what throws people off their commitment is life-altered schedules. This February I was admitted into the hospital with a possible heart attack. I was down for two weeks. I was beyond frustrated because I had just turned forty, wanted to be in the best shape of my life, and I was getting there. I felt like this set me back a bit. But I didn't stay down too long. As soon as I was clear to go back to the gym, I was in there. The following week I was doing two days to give my body a boost!

You must be so committed to your recovery that if anything throws you out of your routine you have to do your best to get back. Making excuses to not get back to your commitment is sure to raise the chances of you going back to your addiction or even prison. You have come too far, friends, to go back. I always look at things like this, you and I were so sold out to our addiction we would make sure we made those drug appointments. Today let's be sold out for our recovery. You're going to be so driven and so committed that no matter what happens, no matter what tries to throw you off, you're going to get back on track. You're going to get back to your commitment to Christ and your new life in recovery.

It's not how we start this journey in recovery; it's how we stay committed no matter what. It's truly how we finish. You hold the key to your commitment level, nobody else. Finish strong. No more excuses! Let's go!

Thoughts & Notes

WHATEVER YOU DO,
WORK HEARTILY, AS FOR
THE LORD AND NOT FOR
MEN

COLOSSIANS 3:23

DAY 14

WALK THE WALK

We have all heard that saying, "don't talk the talk, walk the walk." What that phrase means is your talk should support your walk. What I try to teach people is do more than you say. We have said many times, "This is the last time I go to prison," or, "This is the last time I use drugs or drink." I think we say these things out of comfort for ourselves, not for the people we say it to. It makes us feel better when we hear ourselves say it. This is what I need you to do, stop saying anything. Just do it! Right now, sadly, your words don't mean anything. They have been distorted with lies, broken promises, and years of hurt. The best thing you can do is *just do*. Let your actions do the talking. Don't say you're going to go to church. Just go. Don't say you're going to commit to your new life of being sober and clean. Just do it!

Don't even tell God you want this great relationship with him, just be committed to him and his calling, and do what you know you need to do. If we are all honest with ourselves, we are horrible at keeping our word. But when you just walk your journey of recovery being consistent and faithful, that speaks so much more than saying it. And people see that.

My family came back to me because they saw how committed I was to God and to my new life in recovery. Did I struggle in the process, I sure did, but I stopped talking. If I messed up, I licked my wounds, picked myself back up, and went right back to work. I didn't say it will never happen again, or, "watch me get this right." Nope! I just went back to doing what I was doing. I got back to work on what mattered to me. I kept walking, making the changes that I needed to make. Just walk the walk.

Thoughts & Notes

As EACH HAS RECEIVED A
GIFT, USE IT TO SERVE
ONE ANOTHER, AS GOOD
STEWARDS OF GOD'S
VARIED GRACE

1 PETER 4:10

DAY 15

A HEART TO SERVE

The first time I heard the meaning of this word (Servant) was in the Bible. I always thought it was an outdated word and wasn't for us today. It has been a word that I have kept so close to my heart over the years and here is why. When you truly serve others with your gift that God has given you, there is really something spiritual behind it. We become selfless. In our addiction we were selfish; we were very selfish. It was all about us, what we need, and what we are not getting. One day at my job, I decided to put this word into action. I worked at a gas company and I was in charge of filling oxygen. There were other areas in the warehouse that needed some attention, so as soon as I was done with my work, I moved on to the other task that needed to be done. Keep in mind this was not part of my job. I did this for a few months, just working hard and serving wherever I was needed. The next month I got $1.00 raise. I adopted this same view in the church and in my marriage and family. Just serve them the best I can. But understand when you serve, you serve never to get anything out of it. Not for a pat on the back, you just serve because that's what the Bible teaches us. Can you imagine how the world could be changed if we just served one another instead of worked against each other?

Serving others has allowed me to take the focus off myself and on to others. When you do that, you tend not to think about your addiction. Again, I believe there is something spiritual that takes place in our hearts and lives. We have spent so many years taking from people and even ourselves, we feel good spiritually knowing that we can give back, and that we can do good or even be good. One of my joys I have gotten out of life is not pastoring or even being an author. It's been serving people in our church and even just serving my family the best way I can. I want you to adopt a spirit of serving others. I promise you, friend, it will be just as rewarding for you. Even till this day, I love to clean the bathrooms at the church, because I never want to forget where I have come from and I never want to lose the heart to serve others no matter where God has me.

I believe when we serve others, we also honor God. People miss out on what God has for them because they never adopt the heart to serve. It's more of a, "What can you do for me" or serving with the wrong heart or wrong motives. But you're not that person anymore. You're saved, changed, and renewed. Look for areas to serve in your community, church, and even your job. Always have a heart to serve.

Thoughts & Notes

AGAIN JESUS SPOKE TO
THEM, SAYING, "I AM
THE LIGHT OF THE
WORLD. WHOEVER
FOLLOWS ME WILL NOT
WALK IN DARKNESS, BUT
WILL HAVE THE LIGHT OF
LIFE."

JOHN 8:12

DAY 16

DON'T LET THAT LIGHT GO OUT

I love that the gangbangers and addicts, even those getting out of prison, can feel comfortable to come to our church. I love to see these men full of tattoos, with a hard life, fall on their knees at the altar and ask Jesus to change their hearts to change their lives. It's a beautiful sight to see. You see their lives begin to change. They feel good about their life, and they see God begin to work. That fire is ignited!

But I can also see sometimes, that the fires don't stay lit too long. I would say of every ten men or women that light that fire in their hearts for Christ, only three will continue this journey. Now we can sit here and go back and forth in why that is; relationships, life, or maybe they gave up too soon. I will say this, you have to keep that fire lit every day for Christ, lit every day for your life in recovery. You hold the lighter in your hand.

I can say with a confident heart that I still do things in my life today to make sure that fire is lit for him. Where there days that it could have gone out? Or it needed more gasoline or a replaced wick? Sure, there were! But I recognized where I was at in my life and got that fire lit again. I can't afford for it to go out and you can't either.

You know what happens when it goes out? You're in the dark again, you feel lost again, and you start to feel empty again. There is a possibility that you could go back to your addiction and your old life. You know that fire for Christ has gone out when you complain about everything, when reading your Bible does not excite you anymore. You know that fire is going out when you're in church and in your heart your saying, "Is church over yet?" You will know that fire has gone out when you have stopped learning and growing in your faith and in your new life. This is a heart check I believe for us all. And we have to ask, where have we left ourselves? Where has that fire gone out? Find it again! Get back to what you know you need to start doing. Come to the altar, ask God to forgive you, and get back to work. Seek his heart and light that fire again in your heart and your life. It's hard to find your way if you're in the dark. But remember, you hold that lighter in your hand. Ignite that fire!

Thoughts & Notes

AND HE DID NOT PERMIT

HIM BUT SAID TO HIM,

"GO HOME TO YOUR

FRIENDS AND TELL THEM

HOW MUCH THE LORD

HAS DONE FOR YOU, AND

HOW HE HAS HAD MERCY

ON YOU."

MARK 5:19

DAY 17

TELL SOMEONE

I don't know about you, but I was really excited to tell people about my new life. I was so excited to share what Jesus was teaching me, what he was revealing to me in my life. Some people will listen and some won't. Never let that discourage you in sharing what God is doing in your life.

Most of the time, people think they have to be years clean and sober to even be in a leadership position to share our story. But that is far from the truth, I believe more than ever people want to be inspired. People want to know that there is still hope in this life as we know it. I was shocked when I began to go public with my sobriety and relationship with Jesus how many people would reach out to me and ask me how I was doing it. I believe many people want to have a changed life but they don't know where to start, so they just settle with their current life, no matter how bad it is. The feeling like your tire is spinning in the mud, not going anywhere. Maybe you could be the key to spark something in people's

69

lives for change. I am not saying condemn people to hell, what I am saying is simply share your story with people. Be an ear for the hopeless and a light for those searching. In your new life don't just share your good times, share your struggles as well. I believe what people are looking for is real, genuine faith in Christ. For Christians to be real, raw and transparent. Flakey, fake Christianity never gets us anywhere. Jesus was very clear when he said, "Go tell." So pray that God will open doors for you to share your story with someone, to inspire someone today. In your circle of friends, at your school, or even in your job. Maybe even in prison or jail! Don't limit God in what he will do with your story. Go tell!

Thoughts & Notes

NOW MAY THE GOD OF

PEACE HIMSELF

SANCTIFY YOU

COMPLETELY, AND MAY

YOUR WHOLE SPIRIT AND

SOUL AND BODY BE KEPT

BLAMELESS AT THE

COMING OF OUR LORD

JESUS CHRIST.

1 THESSALONIANS 5:23

DAY 18

MIND, BODY, SOUL

There are three things I measure within myself daily. I do my best to hit every part of these needs. Aim to hit, do not miss! They're important, and here is why. If any of these are off, we will feel it. If all of these are out of place. Guess what? We will be too. That is your Mind, Body and Soul.

Your Mind:

Did you know that what you read can affect the way you think? Even what you listen to can shape how you feel. Social media has made it really easy for us to get off track with our mind. Because if we are not careful, we will read more into what the world is trying to say instead of protecting our mind. Ask yourself today, "What are you reading to shape your mind?" God's word? Good books? With every scroll, social media is shaping your mind. Even sitting down and watching TV for 8 hours, your mind is being shaped. Ask yourself, what are you reading or listening to?

Your Body:

There is something that I believe we can all do to have a healthy and clean bodies. Now Lord knows this is something we can all work on, even myself. I am not saying I eat clean every day, but I do put it into my schedule to work out and give attention to my body. I think how much stress my body deals with. I think about how sometimes our body takes a hit with lack of sleep, stress and worries. You might be saying I can't work out. Ok, then maybe go for a walk or do something outside. Get that heart pumping. For years we damaged our bodies with all the drinking and drugs. Let's feed it good things, and get that body going.

Your Soul:

And last one is your soul. This is your devotion life. Your reading time in God's word, your prayer time, your worship time. This is everything you can do for your spirit, there is a war for it. Evil vs Good! And what you do every day for your spiritual life is up to you. You can't blame the church or the pastor for your own spiritual growth. You have to put things in order for you to grow spiritually.

These three things are very crucial to your recovery and even your life. If any of these are missing, you will know. If all of them are missing, you definitely will know. See what areas you need to work on.

Thoughts & Notes

FOR IF ANYONE IS A
HEARER OF THE WORD
AND NOT A DOER, HE IS
LIKE A MAN WHO LOOKS
INTENTLY AT HIS
NATURAL FACE IN A
MIRROR.

JAMES 1:23

DAY 19

REFLECT

Now that you are half way to the end of the devotion book. Now is time for reflection. How are you doing? What are you learning? How is your recovery going?

These are good question to ask yourself. There is a word that we must see throughout our recovery, and that is progress. This is good because you can see how far you have come, and what you need to work on. Don't use progress for being perfect. You have to use it to see where you are at. If we are not careful, we can get complacent and get used to it, and we never see any growth in our life and in our recovery.

I love this scripture here because it challenges us all, that we aren't just the hearer of the word but we have to be doers. It's like going to a doctor's appointment and they tell you what you need to work on. And if we don't, the risk of illness is a possibility. You can say that is a warning. Did you know we can hear what we need to do for your life to get better, but never apply those things? I tell men and women all the time who come to me for help, I am nobody special. I just learned to apply what I have learned in my Christian life with Christ in my recovery. I have seen it many times that I give people stuff to do and they never apply it to their lives. They hear me, but don't do it.

The Bible is the same way, we know what Christ says but we always want to do the opposite of what he says, then we find ourselves in trouble again. Today I want you to have a time of reflection in your life. Celebrate how far you have come, and get encouraged on the progress you are seeing and get ready for how the next month looks. It can only get better from here, friend! I'm so proud of you.

Thoughts & Notes

BUT WHEN HE SAW THE
WIND, HE WAS AFRAID,
AND BEGINNING TO SINK
HE CRIED OUT, "LORD,
SAVE ME."

MATTHEW 14:30

DAY 20

DON'T LOSE FOCUS

I am all for programs and recovery centers. I believe they are very important and tools we can put in our bag for our life in recovery. Nothing is more heartbreaking then when you hear of men and women going through a year program, they graduate, and there's a celebration when they get home. Then a day later, they are on the streets again, back to their addiction. What happened?

They lost focus when they got out. Life began to happen, and the stress and worries got to them. That anxiety was so high, all they saw was the wind and it got too much for them. They lost sight of who of Jesus was, and they lost sight in who they were. They lost sight in how far they had come.

But there is good news, we don't have to stay there. We too can say, "Save me, Lord." I hope it doesn't get like this for you. You need to stay focused, friend. Not sure if you're in rehab, home, or prison. But you need to keep focused with every-thing you have. Don't lose sight in who Jesus is, or how far you have come in your journey of recovery. You have to be so focused at the task at hand that every day you get up ready to shoot, not to miss but to aim. Aiming for those goals and dreams and your new life.

We all get like Peter and become afraid. We tell ourselves, "Can I really do this?" If we stay there too long and get our eyes off of Jesus, we get our eyes on other things. We get our eyes on what's not im-portant. We take on our fears when we need to put our worries into the hands of a living God. That wind can get intense sometimes, but our God is bigger than anything we face today. And if you do find yourself sinking, just say, "*Lord save me!*"

Reach out your hand. He has never left you. Stay focused, friend. Your life and recovery de-pends on it.

Thoughts & Notes

BUT THE ONE WHO

ENDURES TO THE END

WILL BE SAVED

MATTHEW 24:13

DAY 21

SURVIVE

I am not sure if it just comes with getting older, or if it's just life circumstances. If I really had to be, I am okay with being alone. Not many people can be. Now it has nothing to do with my kids or wife because as I type this, I adore my family and I enjoy their company so much. But if I really had to be, I am okay being by myself. Growing up I really didn't like to be alone. It wasn't until addictions overtook my life that it begin to overtake my mind. You see, even though I was around people in my addictions, I was alone mentally. Alone on late nights walking the streets because I was too drunk to drive. Alone at 5am still binging. Alone in the house when Sasha, my wife, was mad at me for being out all night.

When she left me in 2009, I was really alone. I know what it feels like to be alone, all by myself without money, friends, support, help, words of en- couragement, car, or job. And you know what all this does for me? The times of being alone? The times of hardship of life? It taught me to *survive*, and it taught me that God is my only source and friend. Being by yourself is not a curse, it can be a blessing and we don't even know it. The most times I can feel God speak to me is when I am by myself. Because I am his, and he still whispers in my ear that I am still surviving today. I am okay with not getting invited to a function or event, I am okay not having much friends. In my twenties, I always needed to be around people. In my forties, not so much.

I have learned to be content with who is in my life and who is not. I understand life is a journey, and not many people will go on this journey with me. And you need to be okay with that. You're surviving! And you don't need a whole army to make you feel secured, all you need is Christ.

Keep surviving! Keep moving! And Keep believing for great things for your life

You have all the skills and knowledge you need today to survive. God has placed his spirit in your heart. You will survive whatever comes your way, believe it friend.

Thoughts & Notes

THEN IT SAYS, 'I WILL RETURN TO MY HOUSE FROM WHICH I CAME.' AND WHEN IT COMES, IT FINDS THE HOUSE EMPTY, SWEPT, AND PUT IN ORDER. THEN IT GOES AND BRINGS WITH IT SEVEN OTHER SPIRITS MORE EVIL THAN ITSELF, AND THEY ENTER AND DWELL THERE, AND THE LAST STATE OF THAT PERSON IS WORSE THAN THE FIRST. SO ALSO WILL IT BE WITH THIS EVIL GENERATION."

MATTHEW 12:44-45

DAY 22

TOO FAR TO GO BACK

I think nothing is more heart breaking when men and women work so hard in their recovery, then one day for whatever reason, they break! They drink, they get high again, they are back in the party scene, and all that hard work or even years of sobriety is gone. And you know as well as I do, addicts just don't go small. They go big and fall hard!

Now Lord knows back then in my recovery, I would do this all the time. I would go days with being sober and clean. Then just one random day I would let the stresses of the world get to me and I would use or go back to drinking. And I would do it with no regret and I would fall hard. But something happened in my recovery where I begin to think.

I would think about all the people God put in my life to help me, and all those classes I would go to. All the time and effort that I put into myself to get better. To have a new life of being sober and clean. You see, your recovery is so much bigger than just

89

you. I believe it's those that are around you. My pastor in Oklahoma and even my pastor in New Mexico always made sure that I was okay and that I was doing alright.

It was my kids watching me from the corner of their eyes, holding me accountable, wondering if I was just going to get up one day and leave and not come back again. Once I started to understand that my recovery was more than just me, when life would get hard for me and I got an itch to use, I thought more about who it would hurt and thought more about how far I had come to go back.

Next time you think about using again, don't just think about yourself. Think about those who love you. Next time you think about going back to your old life, think how far you have come and think about how many people have helped you get to where you are at. With God's help, with his spirit, and with your change of thinking, you won't want to go back. You will want to keep moving! God has brought you up out of some messy stuff. He has gotten Hell's grip off of you. You can't go back, stay with it!

Thoughts & Notes

AND WITHOUT FAITH IT
IS IMPOSSIBLE TO PLEASE
HIM, FOR WHOEVER
WOULD DRAW NEAR TO
GOD MUST BELIEVE THAT
HE EXISTS AND THAT HE
REWARDS THOSE WHO
SEEK HIM

HEBREWS 11:6

DAY 23

FAITH

In recovery I heard a lot about trusting God in my new life, but never heard about putting faith in God. I think this makes all the difference in how we see things. Do we trust God? Yes, of course we do. But when we put our faith in him for our recovery and new life, it makes all the difference in the world.

Now more likely as you read this you have nothing, or you are on your way to nothing because of addiction, sometimes we lose everything. Either way, your life is in shambles and you're not sure what to do. Here is why this scripture and faith are important to God and in your recovery.

Our whole lives we tried to please ourselves in what we wanted and needed. We put our faith in drugs to take every pain away, to numb every area of our lives. Now, you have God in your life and your faith is in him alone. The scripture says it's impossible to please God without faith. So you have to not just live your life in faith but in recovery with faith.

So in other words, you have faith that you will be sober and clean. You have faith that your family will come back to you, you have faith you will get out of prison one day. You have faith you will have a great life. In all, you have faith for whatever you're believing God for and have faith he will see you through it. When Sasha and I got back together after being separated for four months, we had faith that God would heal our hearts and restore our relationship. And he did.

Faith is saying even though you don't see how things are going to turn out, you see a road paved to where you need to be. It says, I put my trust in God, in how saved me or restored me, and who loves me! Put your total faith in God today for your recovery and for your life. Take it one step at a time, one day at a time. With faith in your hearts, as the years go by, you can look back and say, "Wow! Look what God did, look how far I have come." And it all had to do with faith.

Thoughts & Notes

THE HEART OF MAN

PLANS HIS WAY,

BUT THE LORD

ESTABLISHES HIS STEPS.

PROVERBS 16:9

DAY 24

WHO IS FLYING YOUR PLANE?

Now there is no secret that I don't like to fly, and over the years I have done my share of flying for the ministry. One time I was sitting down as our plane was boarding and I could smell something burning coming out of the a/c vent. Right away I started to think there is a leak or something. Maybe I should tell the pilot? I then took my head phones off as the plane was about to take off and it's making all kinds of noises, like things are falling apart under my feet. Of course, I want to scream out loud, "Something is wrong with this plane, don't take off!" Can you imagine how silly it would look if I did that, then for me to get out of my seat and knock on the door of the cockpit and say, "Sir something is wrong with this plane?"

All this was playing out in my mind, and then it hit me! This captain knows more about this plane then I do. He trained many hours and went to school about flying. He knows more about this plane then anyone here. He knows what it sounds like, noises it makes, he knows what to look for, he knows eve-rything. What's new to me is old to him. So I decided to sit back and try to relax and trust the pilot and let him do his job, which is to fly the plane and get me to my destination safely. He was flying that plane not me!

Can you imagine if every day we told God how to do his job? We see things in our lives that are out of order. Some of it is our fault and some of it is life. But the noise can be too much, the timing can be hard to adjust to. This is what I do know, God knows what he is doing. He knows where you are at in your life. It's meant to be uncomfortable so you can trust him in your recovery. God is the pilot in your life, and for us to tell him how to fly this plane called life would be foolish.

Hey, I have been there! We want to one day wake up and our life to be somewhat normal. But our whole life has been abnormal for years, and this recovery is not an overnighter. It will take time, and most of it is trusting God where he has you and what he is doing in your life. When you feel discour-aged and want to get up out of your seat and tell the pilot (God) how to do his job, remember he knows more about the plane (life) than you do.

Sit back and let him fly you to your destination. What I also learned being on a plane, especially fly-ing over seas, is that a twenty-two hour flight can be long, but with every minute passing you are closer to your destination more than you know. Be seated! And trust God with your new life. He is the pilot of your life in recovery. As every day passes, you are closer to your breakthrough, closer to your purpose in your new found life.

FOR EVERYTHING THERE

IS A SEASON, AND A TIME

FOR EVERY MATTER

UNDER HEAVEN

ECCLESIASTES 3:1

DAY 25

SEASONS

I don't know about you, but I am winter guy. I don't like anything about the summer. I would be okay if God sent me up north to live. Some people prefer the summer, some the fall. It's a yearly thing, we know that it will start to get hot one day, then one month it will start to get cold. It's seasons, we know they are coming. We do our best to prepare for them, some see it as an excuse to buy more clothes. Hey, I am one of them! It's a time for me to make sure that my sweater game is on point in the winter. But no matter how much we prepare for a season of change, I don't think that we are ready.

Here is what I do know, seasons are that. Just seasons! They don't last forever. Sometimes, they may feel like that, but they don't. It doesn't matter how seasonal things are, they will seem like a very long time. There is that one who loves winter, but then they are ready for things to heat up a bit after that season has taken its course.

Right now as you read this, you don't like the season that you're in. I'm not sure what that is looking like for you, prison or jail time, rehab, or a season of hardships and trial. But it's a season where you don't want to be. You need to tell yourself this season is just for a little while and it won't last forever. It might feel long but this too shall pass. Lord knows in my own personal life I have felt those seasons feel a little bit longer than they should. But I am also reminded that even though seasons change, our God never changes. His peace, strength, comfort, and direction are all the same. And it's in that place that you need to be, not looking at your season, but looking at your God. He will see you through this. He will see that you come out the other end. If we are not careful knowing that seasons are just for a little while, we will let those seasons take control of our lives, and keep us longer then we should, when we need to be focused on the task at hand. So embrace this season and tell yourself it's just for a little while. God is bigger than anything we face, even this season that I am in.

Thoughts & Notes

COMMIT YOUR WORK TO

THE LORD,

AND YOUR PLANS WILL

BE ESTABLISHED

PROVERBS 16:3

DAY 26

FEELINGS VS COMMITMENT

I know serving God can be challenging at times. Even trying to do right and walk a straight line can have its moments. I just turned forty this year and I told myself that I wanted things to change physically and mentally for me, so the gym would be another outlet for me to decompress from my day. I wanted not just to push myself, but for me to be better.

The other day I had to get back to the gym because I been out for a few weeks due to traveling a lot and my schedule was off, my sleep was off, everything was off. Lord knows we all have those days! As I was getting ready to go, I was wrestling with myself and saying, 'I will just go tomorrow." As my ankle passed the pant leg I was trying to tell myself every excuse for why I didn't need to go that day. It got so bad I was driving and still telling myself just not to go. But once I was done working out, I felt better, and I was glad I went and stayed.

I think if we base our life on emotions, we will never get anything done in life. We won't make amends with people we know we need to, we won't read our Bible, we won't pray, or go to church, we won't go to work when we should, we won't finish our goals, and we won't better ourselves. We are emotional people, no doubt! But basing our life on emotions means that we will only move when we feel like it.

Listen to this, when you base your life on emotions you base your life on excuses. But when you base your life on commitment, you base your life on goal accomplishments that you have set for yourself. Problem is, we don't want to put in the work to get there. You see commitment makes you disciplined in areas that we never were.

When you don't feel like doing it, commitment kicks in. It wires something in your brain that, no matter how you feel, you're going to get it done! No matter how you feel, you're going to make sure you will do whatever it takes to get the work done, to get the goal accomplished.

In your recovery, this is the kind of mindset you need to have. If we base our recovery on emotions vs commitment, you will get emotional recovery instead of a committed one. No one said it was going to be easy, but with a heart and mindset to stay committed no matter what, you will see better results. When you say you're committed through this whole process, you're telling yourself that no matter how hard it gets, you're going to finish. No matter how bad of a day you had, when life decided that day was going to squeeze you, what came out of you was commitment and not emotion.

Today, I am sober and clean because I made my mind up that I was going to be committed. Committed to Christ, to his church, to my recovery, and to my new life. Every day I was going to get up and put in work. Nobody had to set an alarm clock for me, nor tell me what I needed to do. I just did it! And you can do this too, friend. But today you must make the choice if you're going to be emotional driven or committed driven. Today make that choice and stick to it no matter what. You can do this, friend!

WE ARE AFFLICTED IN EVERY WAY,
BUT NOT CRUSHED; PERPLEXED, BUT
NOT DRIVEN TO DESPAIR;
PERSECUTED, BUT NOT FORSAKEN;
STRUCK DOWN, BUT NOT
DESTROYED; ALWAYS CARRYING IN
THE BODY THE DEATH OF JESUS, SO
THAT THE LIFE OF JESUS MAY ALSO
BE MANIFESTED IN OUR BODIES. FOR
WE WHO LIVE ARE ALWAYS BEING
GIVEN OVER TO DEATH FOR JESUS'
SAKE, SO THAT THE LIFE OF JESUS
ALSO MAY BE MANIFESTED IN OUR
MORTAL FLESH. SO DEATH IS AT
WORK IN US, BUT LIFE IN YOU

2 CORINTHIANS 4:8-12

DAY 27

BENT BUT NOT BROKEN

This year I was traveling a lot with the book tour for "Letters to My People." I enjoyed being in other churches and sharing the hope we have in Christ and for the things he is doing in my life. Now it's no secret that I do not like to fly, I think my anxiety has gotten better over the years when it comes to flying. But I still have my moments on the plane, in my book I talked about maybe it's normal to have fear of not being in control. I mean think about it. You and I are really trusting a person we never met before, the captain, to fly us 35,000 feet in the air, trapped in a metal tube. But hey, that's just me. Maybe you enjoy flying. One time I was in the air and we had a burst of turbulence. Of course, I was sitting next to the wing, so like any heart felt anxiety person I looked out the window of the plane staring at the wing. That baby was bending up and down, and for one second in my mind I saw it snap right in half right before my eyes and I said, "That's it! Good bye world."

Now we all know turbulence is part of flying, we all know that those wings are tested on every level to withstand what turbulence brings. To our eyes it looks bad, but in the pilot's world it's normal.

Here is what I want to share with you on this day. Your life right now looks like turbulence. You're getting beat on every side, you're all over the place with your emotions. Let's just be honest, maybe today or this week you are a complete mess. But here is something you need to know, God created you! You may bend, but you won't break. You just have to continue to let him be the captain of your life and stay in your seat and trust him with every blow and hit you receive. You have to get your eyes off that turbulence and get your eyes back on God today.

Don't stare out that window too long or you might just get discouraged and stay in a place too long where you didn't attend to stay. I really love this scripture here because it speaks to me even on my hard days. It speaks to me that God made me, and he knows what I have been up against. But he knows I can take it, because he made me. I just need to stay close to him.

He knows that you can take it too, friend, because he made you. He knows what you're up against. I know that you are going to have bad days, we all do. But you cannot give in just because you *think* that you are breaking, then you end up going back to using drugs again or back to drinking.

So whatever is going on in your life right now, I need you to stay in it! I need you to press through. It may look like you're breaking or pressed on every side. But you will get through this. Trust God wherever you are at, and tell yourself, "You can get through this!" You may feel like life is bending you, and even trying to break you. But listen, you will not be destroyed.

"Everyone then who hears these words of mine and does them will be like a wise man who built his house on the rock. And the rain fell, and the floods came, and the winds blew and beat on that house, but it did not fall, because it had been founded on the rock. And everyone who hears these words of mine and does not do them will be like a foolish man who built his house on the sand. And the rain fell, and the floods came, and the winds blew and beat against that house, and it fell, and great was the fall of it."

Matthew 7:24-27

DAY 28

REBUILD ON THE RIGHT GROUND

I think in life we are always building; in our career, our personal life, and spiritual life. At least we should. But how do we know we are building on the right ground? Well the scripture is clear as day. If we are building on the wrong ground, whatever storm (life) comes our way, we will crumble. Can you imagine if builders built houses to last a few years? We would all be in trouble? You have people today that are living in homes that have been around for a very long time. Sure, things shift in a house, but they don't crumble to pieces. If you're on the coast, they build houses not on the ground, but on beams in case a flood comes from a hurricane. Whatever the case is, builders build for the houses to last. If they don't in time we will see how well the house stands after years and storms that come.

In your recovery you have to see that you are building on the right ground. If you don't, you will see things start to fall apart. I think you heard me say this once but I will say it again. Life is life, and

113

it will continue to come at you every single day. Life doesn't say, "Oh wait, they are getting their life in order and cleaned up, let's not pick on them today." Nope! That's not the way it works. It seems like life gets harder and sometimes you have no choice but to think that life is picking on you every day. That's why it's so important that you are building on the right ground. My life today, and I pray yours, too, is to built on the strong foundation of Christ on the right ground.

We think the teachings of Jesus was to hurt us or make us soft. It's actually meant to help us to be better people, to be productive people. To help us from getting involved in sin again, to the destructive patterns of our lives. But when you listen to *his* teachings and apply them to our lives, we are building on the right ground. Will we shake? Sure we will. But if we are building on good ground, no storm (life) can make us crumble. I have seen over time that people who don't build on good ground, like leaves in the fall season soon they will be blown away. And they are back in addiction, they are back in their old life style. They started building well, but for whatever reason they stopped. And that house they were building just sat there. And with seasons of life, it became fragile and brittle then one day it collapsed. The problem was, they never saw it coming. They thought everything was good.

We must never stop building, every day we must continue to build. Into our spiritual life, our personal life and in our recovery. My prayer today is that you will see that you are building things on good ground, or if it is bad that you stopped all together. Whatever the case is, you will begin to build. Your recovery depends on it and so does your life. You can never go wrong listening to the teachings of Jesus. They were meant to help you, not harm you. And see that you always build on good ground. Keep building! Storms (life) come and we don't know when they do. But we need to be ready! Keep building.

IMMEDIATELY THE
FATHER OF THE CHILD
CRIED OUT AND SAID, "I
BELIEVE; HELP MY
UNBELIEF!"

MARK 9:24

DAY 29

CAN YOU BELIEVE

So many people in the Bible had hard times. Some got sick, many struggled, some died. But most all heard about Jesus, his miracles and his teachings. Whenever he went to a town, people flocked to him and needed his help. We can look back into our lives and see how God helped us, big or small he was always there.

But sometimes if we are not careful, we get sucked into the negativity of life and even our own circumstances that we don't ever see a way out of; or even see that we deserve a good life let alone a blessed life. Relapse after relapse, fall after fall, failure after failure. We get to a point in our lives where we say, "I believe, but help my unbelief!"

You start to say, "I believe that one day I can have days, months, years of being sober and clean. I believe that one day my family can be restored. I believe that one day people will look at me and see that I can do good in my life." You might even say,

"I believe one day I can be happy." But then you echo, "Help me with my unbelief!"

I completely understand. In 2009 all I saw was my addiction and what I got myself into. Which was a very deep hole and I just kept digging and getting deeper. I too would think, "I believe, but help me with my unbelief!"

Not sure if your days, months, or years into it but you have to believe! What you see now is not the reality of your future. God has great things for you. He has a great purpose for your life.

People look at me now and see a pastor, author, influencer, maybe even a visionary, and think, "He has a great life." I will say this, even till this day, people have no idea how far I have come or what I have been through mentally and spiritually. I don't have a perfect life, but I do feel I have a surrendered my life to God. Many days I had to push my emotions aside and press through, a lot of tears, sweat and time putting in work every day. Many times, I looked to the sky and said, "God, this is so hard I am not sure I can do this new life of being clean and sober." And yet, here I am. We all have times of unbelief. But if you're a born-again Christian, belief is the main core of our faith. Because our belief is not a world system, it's in Jesus Christ alone! The one who was born, died, buried, then rose three days later. There is so much power in that, so much truth and eternal promises that hell itself can not destroy.

The problem is, we destroy ourselves and our purpose when we have unbelief. And with that I believe we are supposed to live different, not perfect but different!

I wake up every day and say, "Lord, I believe," no matter how things look or how I feel. I am not saying we dismiss our times of doubt. But somewhere in our lives we need to steer that ship back in the right direction and say, "Lord, no matter what I see or feel, today I believe."

You need to know today that you were created for great things, and I need you to start to believe again. Your life has purpose and value. You're a new creation today in Christ with a different belief system than the world. The world sadly operates on emotions. They only do things when they feel good. You operate on God's promises and belief that he loves you so much, to work in your life and your circumstances wherever you are at.

Believe again!

BUT NOAH FOUND FAVOR
IN THE EYES OF THE LORD.

NOAH AND THE FLOOD ⁹

THESE ARE THE
GENERATIONS OF NOAH.
NOAH WAS A RIGHTEOUS
MAN, BLAMELESS IN HIS
GENERATION. NOAH
WALKED WITH GOD.

GENESIS 6:8-9

DAY 30

MAKE A DIFFERENCE

One day after preaching at a church in Pittsburg, I went out to eat with the associate pastor before my flight back home. Now I don't need words of affirmation, but we all know from time to time when those words are spoken, it tells us we are where God wants us to be. Lord knows I have struggled so much in my preaching and communicating ability on Sundays. Like, "Did I give a clear picture of the gospel?" Even to doubting myself. I was like a Moses. "I can't speak clearly. God pick someone else."

But this associate pastor said, "You have a very good way of communicating the Gospel. When you speak, it's like you get people's attention. You do a very good job, like you've been doing it for a long time."

He didn't know this, but I had been struggling within my heart if this was where I was supposed to be. Preaching on Sundays and sharing the Gospel.

But God used him to speak to me. And it was a moment that I said, "Ok God, I hear you." Apparently I have a gift of speaking, a gift of writing. After this book, it will be my second one and I am currently working on two more in hopes that one day two of them will be movie. I am currently trying to open up Alamogordo's first Detox/Recovery home. If God allows this to happen, this will be a place that this city has never seen before.

Every Sunday, I get to watch my daughter sing on the stage for our worship team. I get to hear my son on Wednesday lead the youth group in worship. I get to glance at my beautiful wife ministering to the ladies. And where were all these gifts buried? If we were created in the image of God, why didn't we see them sooner?

Here is why. Mine was in my addiction and wanting to lead my own life. It was buried in my pride and ego. My family's were buried in the world. We all have God given gifts. The problem is, we think we can operate in them while still in the world. We think God will just give them to us while we are still trying to lead our own lives, while we lead a selfish life, instead of letting him lead ours. I wonder how many people today can say they are happy in their jobs. Maybe because they are not operating in their gifts. Hear me when I say this, "I do not like typing nor writing. I don't even like to plan stuff!" Why in the world would God call me to write books or even preach on Sundays, or even be a visionary. It's that gift that was always inside of me the whole time, I just needed to get that junk and distractions out of my life to walk in my calling and gift.

My wife is such an introvert, that's just how she is. Nothing wrong with it. But she operates in her gifting so well when she is called. She is a really good listener and great at giving Godly advice. What's my point? My point of saying all this is not to boast, nor to say look at me or to say my family is better than yours. Trust me we have our faults. It's to say if God can use this family in their imper-fection, he can use you and your gift.

What's your passion? What's burning in your heart? What has God been calling you to do but you have been putting it on the back burner. You have been telling yourself you're not ready, or next year. You're not good enough? That tug on your heart is for you to make a difference in your city or even your family for generations to come. We only get one shot at this thing called life to make things right. To even, somehow in a world that is dark and cold, to make a difference somewhere. To make it a bet-ter place to live.

After this devotion I want you to write down somewhere what you believe God is calling you to do. Ask him to help you discover your gift. When he does, you're going to use it for him and to bring him glory.

Today, get out of the water that is drowning your calling and begin to discover it. Because when you

know what you were called to, you find your purpose, and you find you and you begin to walk with
God.

Thoughts & Notes

BUT YOU, TAKE COURAGE! DO NOT LET YOUR HANDS BE WEAK, FOR YOUR WORK SHALL BE REWARDED."

2 CHRONICLES 15:7

DAY 31

KEEP THOSE HANDS UP

I don't like the word "quitting". But for this last day of my devotions, I want to use the phrase, "throwing in the towel." Any boxer will tell you when they see that white towel in the ring it means the fight is over. For the one dominating the fight it's a win. For the corner that threw it, it means defeat! Most of the time you will see the fighter throw up his hands like, "Why did you do that?" Maybe they feel like they had some more fight in them or maybe the corner will see they put their hands down and they were taking too many shots to the head. Whatever the case, the fight is now over.

I wish I could say that your life will be easy being clean and sober. But it won't. As a matter of fact it could get harder for you. Life doesn't stop throwing punches just because you're getting on your feet. Sometimes life don't even let you catch your breath. It loves to take those body shots. But that's why, no matter how tired you feel, how discouraged you feel, how many bad days you have in a month, how

127

many times you get hit in the face with life, you need to keep those hands up. What I like about this whole illustration is *man* is not in your corner. God is!

If I can count how many times man has told me, "Pastor I am in your corner, I will never hurt you, you have my full support." Then as fast as they said it, they are gone. They left that towel hanging on the rope. But God is in that corner. He is your cut man, hype man, and coach. He won't throw in that towel. Sometimes we are the ones that look at him and say, "Throw the towel, I give up!" And we walk out of the ring of life, never looking back and turning away from God and our purpose. If you don't keep those hands up, if you let them drop, you will get hit so much that you will feel in your heart there is no choice but to give up.

I don't know about you, but let me speak this last piece of word into your heart. If you're going to keep battling, you need to train your mind and spirit *daily*. Notice how I put that in emphasis. People give up because they stopped working on themselves. They stopped the training. They think one Sunday service or one Bible study, one worship is going to get them by and it's not. The devil does not sleep, nor does he stop coming after us. He wants to destroy your life and your purpose and your legacy. His main job is to confuse, disrupt, and make sure you destruct on every level. He loves to see you defeated. How about we get in that ring toe to toe with his legion of demons with those scriptures in our hearts, full of the spirit of God and keep those hands up. Swing when we need to, giving that devil a black eye. It's not how many punches you can take, it's that you're still standing with your hands up, taking those shots.

You are now a threat to him because he doesn't have you in darkness and sin anymore. You're in the light and you are a child of God. He knows you're a threat, and he will do whatever he can to see that you will fall. Nothing in my life surprises me anymore; the betrayal, the hurtful words people speak, and the fiery darts that people or the devil throws at me. I know I have a huge target on the front *and* back of me. But I have to stand in that ring with my hands up, and I am encouraged, because God is with me no matter who is around or who has left. I want you to read this slowly:

2 TIMOTHY 4:14-17
Alexander the coppersmith did me great harm; the Lord will repay him according to his deeds. Beware of him yourself, for he strongly opposed our message. At my first defense no one came to stand by me, but all deserted me. May it not be charged against them! But the Lord stood by me and strengthened me, so that through me the message might be fully proclaimed and all the Gentiles might hear it. So I was rescued from the lion's mouth.

Did you read this? He will stand with you and give you strength in whatever he has called you to do. You, my friend, just need to stay in this thing called life. And you need to stand there strong, knowing God is in your corner when nobody else will be. Stand there with your hands up! Let's go! Keep going! You are made for great things!

ABOUT THE AUTHOR

Anthony Torres was born in Altus, Ok. He grew up in Las Cruces, Nm. And now resides in Alamogordo, Nm with his wife Sasha Torres. He is the father of 4 wonderful kids. He is the Pastor of MountainVIEW Church, a Church that is outreach driven to REACH1 in its community, he also the founder of "New Life Recovery" His heart is to see people set free from Addictions. Connect with him on Social media.

Facebook@reach1forHOPE
Instagram@recovered_addict09

Anthony and his wife Sasha have been the Pastors of MountainVIEW Church since 2015 in Alamogordo, NM. They started off with only 20 people in attendance. Today 2021, they have over 300 people that call MountainVIEW Church home. And still growing today. Their hearts are to minister Jesus to broken people, speaking about the love, forgiveness, and rebuilt lives that Jesus offers.

Anthony loves street ministry, and creating a movement to reach1 on the streets with outreach in the city monthly.

Sasha is the overseer of women's ministry and Calcutta Mercy Café that sponsors children monthly in Calcutta, India for an education. If you like to write Anthony you can send letters to

MountainVIEW Church
1300 Cuba AVE
Alamogordo, NM 88310:
Attention Anthony Torres.

Or you can email him at
Anthony@mvagalamo.com.
Check out the churches website at
www.mvcalamo.com

If you would like Anthony to speak at any event or come speak in the prisons email him at: Anthony@mvagalamo.com

CHECK OUT ANOTHER

BOOK FROM THE AUTHOR:

"Letters to my People"
Thoughts of a Recovering Addict.

www.recoveredaddict21.com or on Amazon

GET

YOUR

COPY

TODAY!

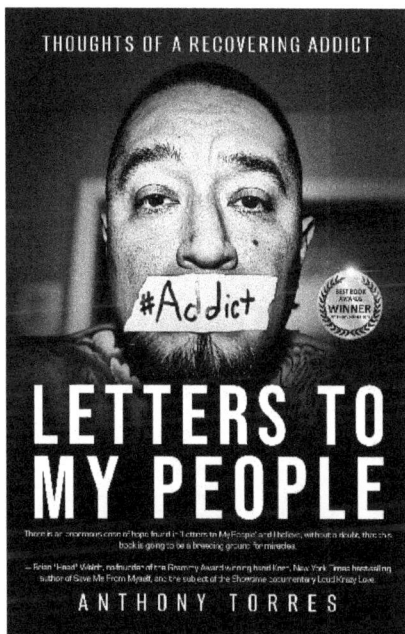

www.ingramcontent.com/pod-product-compliance
Lightning Source LLC
Chambersburg PA
CBHW060511030426
42337CB00015B/1839